William Bolcom

Concerto in D
for Violin and Orchestra

Violin and Piano Reduction

In Three Movements
I.   Quasi una Fantasia
II. Adagio non troppo ma sostenuto
III. Rondo – Finale

Duration: *ca.* 20 minutes

World Premiere: Sergiu Luca, violin, Saarbrucken Radio Orchestra,
Dennis Russell Davies conducting, June 3, 1984.

ISBN 0-634-00054-3

EDWARD B. MARKS MUSIC COMPANY / EXCLUSIVELY DISTRIBUTED BY HAL•LEONARD® CORPORATION

7777 W. BLUEMOUND RD. P.O. BOX 13819 MILWAUKEE, WI 53213

Program Note

The first movement is a fantasy-form in the strict sense it had in the Classical era, in which alternation of types of music depends primarily on timing for its success. The opening ostinato leads to the soloist's entrance in an expansive mood; this quickly gives way to a macabre waltz *(Molto allegro)* which metrically modulates to a fast gigue. The material is restated in the dominant; musical passages of grand-style tragedy soon follow, and it is the tension between the tragic and the more positive opening moods that animates and builds the form of the piece.

The solemn second movement, in 5/4, is in memory of a close friend; the long adagio line includes a ghostly discourse between the soloist and an offstage D trumpet. This leads without pause into the Rondo-Finale, in which the influence of the late jazz violinist Joe Venuti is most apparent. Several popular styles are alternated rondo-fashion until the *stretta* at the end, where the soloist's brilliant passagework ends the Concerto.

WILLIAM BOLCOM

Full score and orchestra parts are available on rental from:

Theodore Presser Company
One Presser Place
Bryn Mawr, PA 19010
Tel (610) 525-3636 • Fax (610) 527-7841

Orchestration is scored for Solo Violin and the following instrumentation:

2 Flutes (2 dbl. Piccolo)
2 Oboes (2 dbl. English Horn)
2 Clarinets in Bb (1 dbl. Eb Clarinet, 2 dbl. Bass Clarinet)
2 Bassoons (2 dbl. Contrabassoon)

2 Horns in F
2 Trumpets in Bb (1 dbl. Trumpet in D)
Tenor Trombone
Bass Trombone

Timpani
2 to 3 Percussionists (Snare Drum, Wood Block, Crotales,
  Glockenspiel, Chinese Cymbal, Hi-Hat, Small Cymbal,
  3 Tom-Toms or Timbales,Suspended Tambourine,
  Small or Medium Tam-Tam or Gong)

Harp
Piano (dbl. Celeste)

Strings (full size or chamber orchestra)

for Sergiu Luca

Concerto in D
for Violin and Orchestra

I. Quasi una Fantasia

William Bolcom
(1983)

NB: Accidentals obtain only throughout a beamed group: = all A♭

In music with key signature, traditional practice applies.

First Publication 1998

Molto Allegro ♩. = 72

Vivace (Lo stesso tempo)

♪ = 𝅗𝅥.

Faster than Tempo II, 𝅗𝅥. = 84 approx.

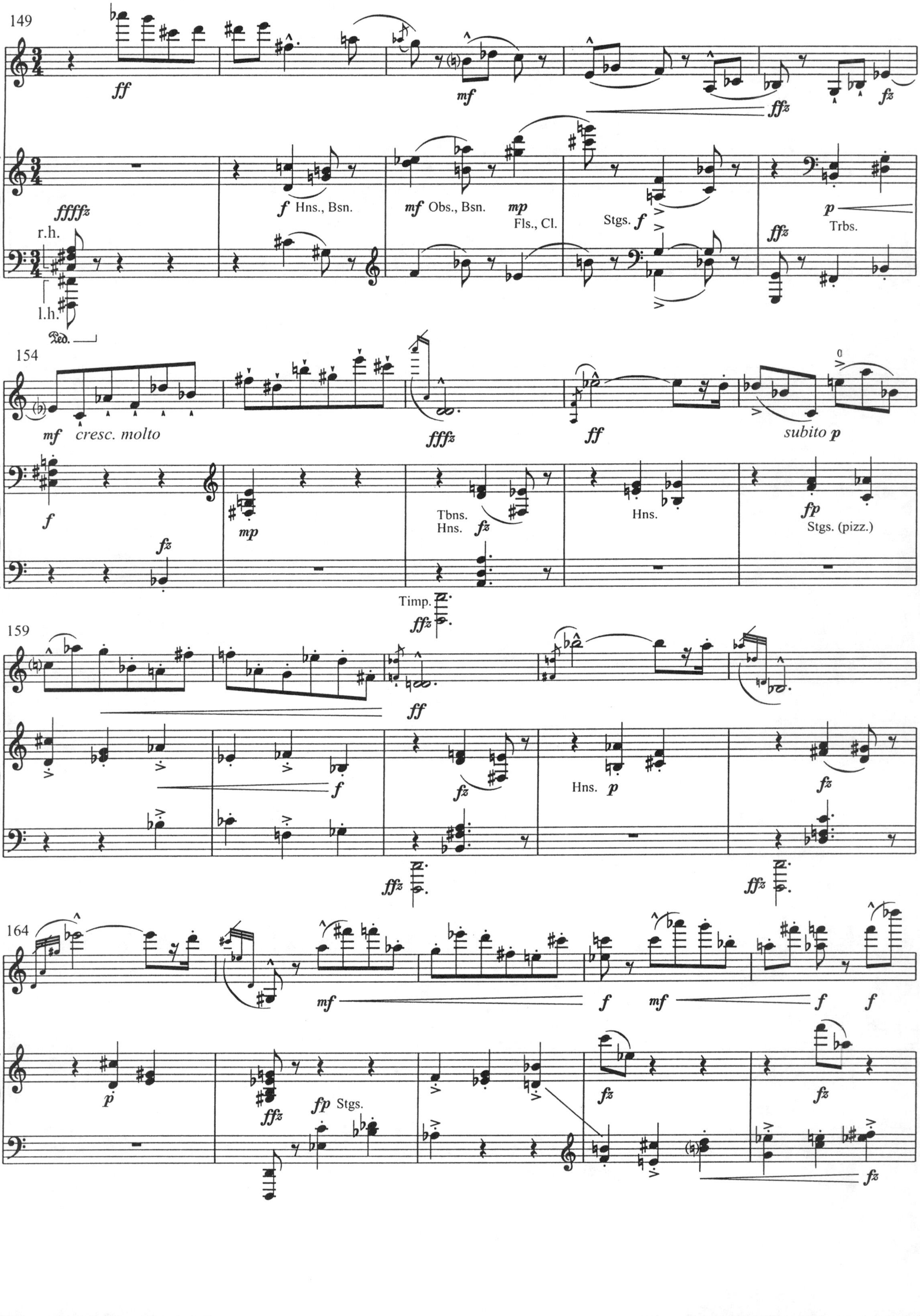

* ⅄ = short pause

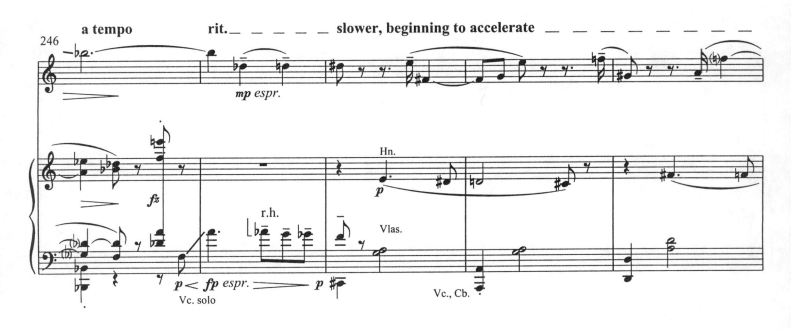

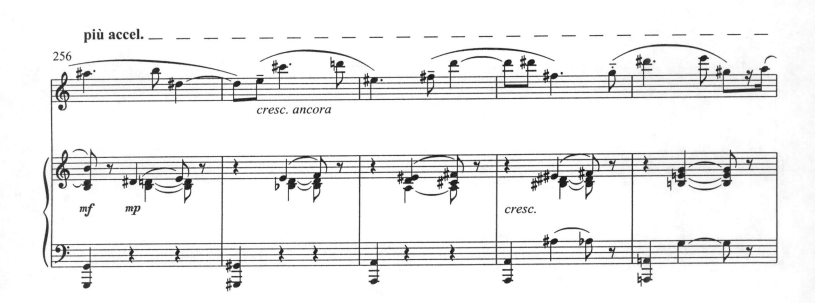

* The tempo should relate to the foregoing but can be as slow as ♩. = 60.

Sept. 5, 1983
Ann Arbor, MI

II. Adagio non troppo ma sostenuto

attacca

III. Rondo–Finale

December 4, 1983
Ann Arbor, Michigan